Legal & Disclaimer

The information contained in this book is not designed to replace or take the place of any form of medication or professional medical advice. The information in this book has been provided for educational and entertainment purposes only.

The information contained in this book has been compiled from sources deemed reliable, and it is accurate to the best of the Author's knowledge. However, the Author cannot guarantee its accuracy and validity so cannot be held liable for any errors or omissions. Changes are periodically made to this book. You must consult your doctor or get professional medical advice before using any of the suggested remedies, techniques, or information in this book.

Upon using the information contained in this book, you agree to hold harmless the Author from and against any damages, costs and expenses, including any legal fees, potentially resulting from the application of any of the information provided by this guide. This disclaimer applies to any damages or injury caused by the use and application, whether directly or indirectly, of any advice or information presented, whether for breach of contract, tort, negligence, personal injury, criminal intent, or under any other cause of action.

You agree to accept all the risks of using the information presented inside this book. You need to consult a professional medical practitioner in order to ensure you are both able & healthy enough to participate in this program.

Contents

Introduction

I want to thank and congratulate you for downloading the book, *"Cracking the Internet Millionaire Code: 20 Passive Income Ideas Online to Help You Create the Lifestyle You Truly Desire."*

This book contains proven strategies on how you can make passive income online as a way of building the life you have always desired. Sometimes it is never enough to just have an office job without other sources of income and is the reason I introduce you to the idea of online income which is a path towards success.

It is possible that you may have heard the idea at some point in time but have never had a chance to know exactly how to go about and this is the reason why this book is for you. It will act as your best guide as it opens you up to the world of online income ensuring that you fully understand all of its aspects. There is actually so much you need to know for you to be able to succeed in this field all of which have been well explained in the book.

The idea of making as much money as you would wish online is as true as you would wish it to be and many have tried and have never regretted it. The best thing is that there is something for everyone and you don't really have to be skilled or qualified academically for you to gain what everyone else is.

The most important thing is that you learn how to get the best jobs or ways you can make online income and those should be things that you understand and that you will produce the best once at it.

The world is full of possibilities and all one needs to do is find those possibilities because as you know nothing comes easy in life. Online income may sound as an easy way to make money but much will be required from you including hard work, determination, patience, persistence, honesty and so much more.

The road to financial independence requires you to have multiple sources of income and the internet has provided ground for that. You should actually make this opportunity a life changing one because there is nothing to lose and much of what you need to sacrifice is your time.

With the growing economy you will realize that people are expanding their businesses in different ways and the internet is taking all of that. Once you begin working online you will realize that it is the best thing that could have happened to you because it comes with so much benefit.

Every chapter of this book has been written in a way that ensures you get to learn of most if not all of the things that you need to know about online income. It begins by giving you a deeper understanding of what online income is and some of its benefits, it also enlightens on how to identify and avoid online scams, common mistakes made when it comes to online jobs, twenty main methods of making income online and so much more. It is my hope that you will enjoy reading it and that it will benefit you fully.

Grab Free Books Here

From time to time, I would highlight to my readers some interesting books which I found on Kindle. Subscribe to our newsletter to receive free bestselling kindle books recommendation delivered to your inbox daily. You can subscribe to our newsletter by clicking on the link below:

http://giveaway.kindleheaven.com/index.php/kindle-free-book/

It is 100% free and there will not be a single spam email. Just pure sharing of good books with my readers.

Please also like our facebook page below to get recommendation on good books to read for the day.

https://www.facebook.com/Kindle-Heaven-1651266215134798

Follow us on Twitter to get tweets on worthwhile books

https://twitter.com/KindleHeaven

Chapter 1: Understanding The Basics Of Online Income

Understanding How Online Income Works

The first and most important thing to do before venturing into anything in life; is getting a deeper understanding of what it is all about and this is the main reason why I have this part of the book for you. Regardless of age, gender, situation one can work online because there is something for everyone and it is the best place to make passive income.

With online jobs one is their own boss and you get to choose your own working hours. What could be better than this, and as mentioned there are all kinds of things you can engage in and all you need to is find one that is suitable. There is normally no prior experience required and once at it all you need to do is work really hard and give your all to increase productivity.

Am sure you have ever heard of the idea that the internet is a great way to make some money which is true but how to it should be your key concern. All you are good at including writing, photography, data entry can be turned into some very good money online. If you want to become a successful online entrepreneur, then you really need to research on how best you can achieve this.

As you may know so many companies prefer to outsource their work instead of having in house staff and this is the reason why you can find any kind of job online and have the pleasure of working from the comfort of your house. There are all kinds of people online and you need to know chances are that as a beginner you are likely to encounter scams because there are just as many scams as there are legit reasons. It is therefore best to know how to identify and avoid such, you need not worry much about that because it has been well covered in the book and you read that later.

As easy as it may sound, you should also know that it being a road to riches it also requires determination, hard work and perseverance. From time to time the internet has always been used for all kinds of interests but the most has been for business ventures and this is what created a path for online jobs. Online jobs may have some disadvantages but the benefits override them.

As compared to other jobs, online jobs are quite interesting and also very beneficial and it gives you ground to practice your skills and also acquire new ones. Once you learn how to identify the legit jobs online then you will be on a path to making millions, literally.

The best thing you can and should always do is to think creatively on ways in which you can adapt your skills and qualifications to the available online jobs. Always have an open mind in whatever you try and specialize on one thing instead of jumping from one job to another.

Benefits of Online Jobs

This is a very interesting part of the book it being a chance to get to know of all the major benefits and advantages of online jobs. It is meant to act as your source of motivation and will help you make your decision regarding your thought of making passive income through online jobs.

It is always very important to know what is in store for you before putting your efforts and resources into anything. Online jobs come with a number of benefits all of which am sure are exactly what every single person is looking for in a job. You should actually know that online jobs are the best bet for working at home employment opportunity and is a gold mine for anyone who is looking to make passive income or just work full time at home. These benefits and advantages are as explained below:

- With online jobs one is able to work at the comfort of their homes and this is something almost every single person would wish for. The only thing that one requires to make money online is a working computer and a good internet. As we always say "east or west home is best" which is true because personally I would give anything to be able to work at home which is a very comfortable environment and chances are that your productivity will be high.

- Another very important thing about online jobs is that it is open for everyone and it also has numerous opportunities. As mentioned, anyone can venture into online jobs and do something they always love doing making an income in the process. You actually get to do what you want and will therefore not get stuck in job you don't enjoy for the rest of your life. All you need to do is look through different sites that offer online jobs and find that one thing that is good and comfortable for you. Sometimes you don't really have to live a life that situations put you into explore the internet and change your life forever.

- With online jobs one is also a boss of themselves, no one will be there to supervise you or confirm if you are at work or if you are doing whatever it is their way. When it comes to online jobs you have the freedom to work at your own time and at your own pace as long as you ensure you are making progress and are also being productive. You might find that there are a number of people who have anxiety issues and working under pressure at an office job does them no good and it is therefore best for them to work online where no one will pass criticism or push them around. Under this environment they end up being more productive.

- Another great thing about online income is that one gets to take much of what they earn home because taxes are only taken from your net pay and you will always have enough to spend and also pay all your bills. Real jobs come with so many deductions and at times you end up not having enough to spend and take care of your family. One can also combine the two jobs and at the end they will have more than enough.

- There is also the idea of flexibility and one can be able to handle different types of online jobs as a way of increasing their income. It is however advised that you should not take up so much that you won't be able to handle. What is important is the ability to perform greatly as this is the only way you will grow as a person and also be able to grow your business.

- It is also a place where you will utilize your skills to the maximum and also get to learn new skills. This way you grow as a person and you will end up being more productive as you will handle more projects or even have more ideas of expanding your business. You will find that great entrepreneurs grow from online experience because this is a field where you encounter different people with all kinds of thoughts.

- When one decides to only focus on online income alone they will be working at home and this means more time spent with family. As a woman you will be able to take care of your children especially when they are really young and they will grow very healthy. It will also be a chance for you to handle all the family issues without worrying about your job.

- There are totally no limitations in terms of age, skills or anything. Anyone one can handle online jobs and make an income as long as they know what they are doing.

- There are usually very minimal distractions when working online because chances are that you are mostly working at home or at a quiet place. With fewer distractions you will be in a position to focus and this increases your productivity. With an office job there are all kinds of distractions, unnecessary interruptions, unimportant meetings all of which you can avoid if you decide to work from home.

- One also gets to save on a lot of costs when they decide to do online jobs alone and this could be on office clothes, transportation, lunch and so much more. All these can go into your savings and investments and you will be on a path towards financial independence.

- It is also good to know that online jobs are the easiest way to make money and one can make as much as they want because they are the ones to decide when and how long to work. You get paid depending on how hard you are willing to work and actually the harder you work the more you earn.

Chapter 2: Chartering Your Own Financial Destiny

Achieving Financial Independence

Financial independence is that state when an individual has sufficient personal wealth to live without necessarily working actively for their basic necessities. When one attains financial independence it means that they have assets which generate income that is greater than their expenses.

To get there one has to learn how to manage their career and investments so that they won't have to work again. All these include creating multiple sources of income and the best way to do this is by venturing into online jobs.

There are those who achieve financial independence through investing and saving for a long period of time while others build businesses that will always be generating income for them. You should never focus on the thought that financial independence is only for the rich because anyone can get there as long as they learn how to.

Just as you will need an innovative mind to make online income that same skill is required to achieve financial independence. All it takes is following through the wealth generating habits and they will make your dream of becoming financially independent a reality.

Many of us live life not knowing what they really want out of it or without any specific goals which is not a good way to live. Without a vision you won't be able to make any progress and won't also improve yourself as a person. With financial independence you won't have to worry about financial constraints and its benefits are numerous.

This book focuses on enlightening you on the idea of online income which is great because it is a good way to attain financial independence through making passive income.

Financial independence means different things to different people but whatever you think it means to you the ways of getting there are specific. It isn't something that happens overnight and therefore requires hard work and patience. The reason I have this part of the book is that it will help you know how important it is to work towards building your financial security.

It takes a lot and once you begin working towards building online income then you make things easier for yourself. In whatever business you decide to venture into this knowledge will take you to higher levels of success. You should also not think of financial independence in terms of retirement as it can come earlier on. Time is always your most valuable asset and the earlier you begin to work towards that the better.

<u>Steps to Achieve Financial Independence</u>

As already mentioned it takes a lot to get there because being financially independent is something big and also very great. There are specific steps that you should take for you to attain it all of which are very well explained in this chapter.

Once this idea clicks early then you will understand why it is important for you to work hard to be financially independent. One thing you should put in mind is that the effort only comes from you and no one else. And since you are reading this it is proof enough that you are ready to try the most important step to take is always educating yourself on all that you need to do. All these are well explained below:

- **Goal setting:** Any success comes with being able to set goals; this allows you to have clarity on where you are and where you want to be. It is also an opportunity to strategize on how best you can achieve your dreams. With goal setting you will easily work towards a certain objective and will know how to allocate resources to your priorities.

- **Investing wisely:** This is a key aspect when you are striving to attain financial independence because it is also a path towards creating multiple sources of income. It is not always about investing but making wise investments those which will at the end grow your money.

- **Spending wisely:** As they always say the best way to double your money is to fold it and put it back. This is where you should get the idea of the importance of spending wisely. Try to focus on your needs rather than wants and this way you will know where to put your money.

- **Risk taking:** Risk taking comes with being open minded and having the courage to try out new things because you never know where your true success. It also opens you to more possibilities in life and this you will grow as a person and will also identify areas that you should best invest in. when you think of venturing into online jobs you do it as this is the only way that you will know whether it is a good idea.

- **Budgeting:** Budgeting is also another very important thing to do because it will keep you on track with your income and you will avoid unnecessary spending and will also know where your money goes and whether it has been put into good use. Through budgeting one also has enough to save or even invest.

- **Saving:** No matter how much you earn you should always exercise the habit of saving, with savings you will always have enough for future emergencies and it is also an opportunity for you to make investments.

- **Clearing debts:** Debts are always a draw back to your success and it is best that you avoid them if possible or clear them as soon as possible. If you don't then you will find that they increase from time to time and you will end up paying a lot for something that didn't make a big difference in your life. It is also advised that you should begin paying the high interest debts first.

Chapter 3: Identifying Online Scams and How to Avoid It?

If it sounds too good to be true, it probably is...

It is difficult for many people to differentiate between a legitimate online job and those that are scams. As a beginner it is important for you to understand that scam jobs have increased in number and they are as many as legitimate ones, this has really made it hard for one to tell the difference between what is real and what is scam.

Don't rush yourself into investing all your savings and put all your efforts and valuable time before understanding what you are getting yourself into. Be open minded about everything because scammers know how hard people are looking for online jobs and they will do all they can to ensure that a large number of people fall into their trap.

When you come across many scam jobs there is no need to quit but rather continue searching for jobs in the right way. There is a saying that goes, "When the deal is too good, think twice" and this is what you should follow through at all times.

Scammers usually know how difficult it is to find job and that is why they trick people by marketing and promoting where legitimate employers and organizations do. Scammers make many promises and usually want you to pay for a certain service before you begin to work.

Many people want the chance to be able to work and make extra cash online and it is therefore important for you to learn, know and understand how they can be able to avoid scam. Most scam jobs have similar features as those for legitimate jobs and this makes them to appear legitimate and it is therefore of importance for you to be keen for you to note the difference.

There is no one who is smart to be scammed and the only thing you should do is focus on how you can keep yourself from being scammed. As an individual with knowledge you should know what to expect and this will help you to be at lesser risk of being scammed.

Worry not because this part of the book is meant to enlighten you on how best you can be able to detect scam. The following are different guidelines and ways that can help you to be able to differentiate between a legitimate job and a scam one:-

1) Sometimes you might be offered a job without an application or any discussion with the company.

2) Scam firms usually ask for personal information such as driver's license or even social security number.

3) Some scam jobs also present their jobs by preying upon dreams or desires for a simple life. They do this by showing expensive cars, huge payout checks, big houses etc.

4) There are some scam firms that have not clearly explained their salary details. They don't clearly describe if you are to be paid a fixed rate or hourly rates.

5) Some scam firms are not very specific on what they are looking for in terms of skills, qualification, experience and expectations.

6) Scam jobs can promise you a high pay for doing less work. As explained earlier, "When the deal is too good, think twice" and it is of importance for you to know if the pay is exaggerated or is a higher pay for the work you are doing.

7) Many online scam jobs also claiming or promising what your income might be in terms of per day, weekly or monthly.

8) You receive unprofessional emails that have spelling errors, punctuation errors or even capitalization errors.

9) If you search up the company it doesn't add up or you find a company that has almost the same name.

10) Some scam jobs also want to steal your skills and ideas and they never state precisely how they are going to

help you grow and also how they are going to market/advertise your business or company.

How to Avoid Online Scams?

After you have grasped all the ways you can use to differentiate between a legitimate and a scam online job, the next step is to know how you can avoid these scams:-

1) **You should be aware:** It is of importance to keep in mind that the internet is not a safe place. There are many of tricks scammers can use to get your money and you should therefore do some research and verify if a certain job is genuine or not. Don't trust anyone or any website.

2) **Call and confirm if their number is really working or not:** You must look for a working or functioning phone number. It is of importance for you to call and

confirm if someone can answer the phone or if it will go to voicemail.

3) **Google or search the company's name:** This is the best way of researching and learning more about the company. By searching for the company's name you will be able to access their website and read reviews of people that were happy or unhappy with the company. If there are many complaints then that is a sign that the company is a scam. You can also just Google the company's name and see if anything negative shows up.

4) **Check the contact information:** If you have found large online company, most of them usually have multiple locations but some of them can hide their headquarters location for security purposes. For small companies, try to look for a real address that you can use to ship things other than the P.O. BOX. Also specific sites can have contact information from other independent sites that are actually legitimate.

5) **Search the company's name on scam.com's forums:** Scam.com is a great internet resource and a large forum where people usually complain about firms that have scammed them. If you see multiple

complaints about a given company then that is a red flag. You can also use other sources that are legitimate to search and ensure if a certain online job is legitimate or not.

6) **Trust your gut:** If a deal sounds too good to be true, think twice. There is always a part inside us that will see the red flags. Don't let desperation to mislead you into being scammed because you can simply trust your gut in knowing what is scam and what is legitimate.

7) **Copyright:** Any online job that is legitimate must have an up-to-date copyright. If the company's website has been around since 1989, then you can look for the "copyright-company name- 1989 to 1999." If the company's website still says "copyright 1989" then it means that it is not clear if the company is still in business or not.

Chapter 4: Twenty Main Methods To Make Money Online

This is the most important part of the book as it introduces you to the main methods through which you can make money online and this is meant to make your start easier. It allows you to have a rough idea of where you can start from having made a decision to embark on the online income journey.

This will help you make money in your spare time or even full time. It is however not all there is in online jobs meaning that there are plenty of other ways in which you can make money but these are the best options and am sure you will find something suitable.

A good number of people are out to look for ways in which they can make money through the internet and this includes stay at home mums, students and even those working.

First of all you should know that working online is not an easy thing and for you to be successful you have to work really hard and also take your job seriously. There is no indicator as to how much you will earn as it all depends with you, how hard you work and how great you perform. As already mentioned the internet has all kinds of scams and the knowledge on identifying and avoiding them is very important.

The twenty main methods are as explained below:

1. Online Surveys

This is a very popular way for anyone to make money online and you can do this by filling out online surveys in their spare time. The best thing is that research companies are always recruiting new members to answer surveys and also test new products. You need to know that membership is free and once your membership is complete you start earning points by completing online surveys and this can be done anytime and anywhere via laptop, PC, cell phone, tablet or Mobile App. The legit online survey sites include Toluna, Swagbucks, Vivatic, My survey, Survey Bods etc. these are however things you should do during your free time as it doesn't earn you a lot.

Passive Income Potential (Moderate): Not much if you are doing it by the minute because it takes time to complete surveys. However, some websites pay you to recruit new survey takers and you get to earn a percentage of the surveys that they complete.

2. Review Websites And Apps

If you are one of those people who are perfect web browsers then it is time you turn those skills as a paying job. There are companies which help people with mobile apps and websites improve them and as an outsider you can be paid to visit the websites and mobile apps and give your perspective. You get to review their functionality and give out helpful feedback rating them based on experience. If you have a flexible schedule, good internet connection, mobile devices, up to date computer and this is something you are interested in then you are good to go. You should try out usertesting.com which pays people to review all types of websites and every review takes about 20 minutes.

Passive Income Potential (Low): Not much passive income potential as you have to go through each site professionally and leave constructive reviews. Plus it is very time consuming because you will need to spend some amount of time on each site which can add up significantly. Nevertheless, this is still an easy source of income for those who are just dabbling their feet in the online world.

3. Write And Publish A Kindle EBook

If you love writing then this should your thing because you can actually publish an eBook and make money. You should therefore know that the Kindle app is available in a number of devices including ipads, smartphones, laptops which makes your global market huge. The trick is writing on a topic that will capture the interest of many and should be helpful and well written because your target audience are the ones to pay you. Once you have it published and people love and benefit from it then you will be on a path to making very good money. To succeed with eBooks you have to create something of value and also write non-fiction. Another important thing you should focus on is having your cover designed very well for your book to stand out.

Passive Income Potential (High): As long as your kindle book remain published, there is a chance that book lovers may still buy your book. Plus, there is an added advantage when you publish on kindle because you are working with a respectable company, Amazon. When your book is on promo or countdown days, Amazon will also help promote your book to subscribers.

4. Affiliate Marketing

Affiliate marketing is advertising through the internet and it allows online business to affiliate themselves using affiliate programs. This is where a business rewards one or more affiliates for every visitor brought by the affiliate's marketing efforts.

If you have a blog or website or a good presence on social media then you can use that to promote companies, services, offers online and products. There are some specific things that you really need to put in mind all of which will help you grow as an affiliate marketer and these include the idea of helping the customers rather than selling. You should always focus on making the customer understand why the specified product or service is great for them and not just pushing them to buy. It is a great way to make money as it is so hands off and can also be automated easily delivering great profit margins.

Passive Income Potential (High): Initial stages may be difficult but once your niche sites rank for its keywords or you have a ppc campaign that does not require much tweaking, the income is pretty much passive

5. Blogging

Professional blogging is considered as one of the best known ways that one can make income online. With your own blog you can earn money advertising or even room your own content. There are actually numerous free and also very good blog sites where one can easily set up their blog and you begin by writing interesting things and then when you have a good number of visitors then you begin putting online ads.

Much of the skills required include a good command on language, familiarity with basic coding and some other technical stuff like SEO and also the ability to write in an interesting way. Usually blogging can bring varied amounts of money depending on the web traffic that you receive and also the monetization strategy you choose to adopt.

Passive Income Potential (Moderate): Blog may take some time to cultivate before you can make passive income out of it. Once you have built your own brand and authority, your site will start ranking for long tail keywords. You will be able to make money from advertisers and Google Adsense.

6. Teaching Online

One can also be a teacher online as you can choose to teach anything depending on your skill and expertise. Once you market yourself well you will be in a position to offer lessons to perspective students. A good place to begin from is the skill-share which will allow you to be an online teacher. All you do is register and then create courses on the subject you are good at and this could be anything including cooking, different languages, designing etc. another important site you should know of is Udemy where you sell your courses and get paid any time a student takes the online course that you developed. This can be quite interesting because you will be sharing something you are good at and chances of earning a lot are high.

Passive Income Potential (High): You just need to teach your course once and you can repurpose it into ebook, audio course, etc and publish those to various merchant websites to help you sell your lessons. Earning potential can run into tens of thousands of dollars for one on one lessons.

7. Virtual Assistant

One can also make a lot of money by being a virtual assistant, who is a person that provides services to organizations, companies or individuals online. It is a very good work at home experience and is all open to everyone as there are all kinds of opportunities. There is so much to virtual assistance than just administrative assistance as the field is broad. The rates are usually very high and you can find that it ranges from $15-$100 depending on the skill you are willing to offer.

Passive Income Potential (Low): Not much as you are paid by the hour. However, it is possible to outsource your work to those who are willing to do the same work for less so that you can focus on getting more orders.

8. Review Music

Another way to make money online is by reviewing music online and all you need to do is sign up and listen to a track, rate it and write an honest review about it. When you become experienced by making more reviews then the more you will charge.

Passive Income Potential (Low): Knowledge of music is very specialized and so this income source is not replaceable anytime soon. However, you are only paid for each piece of music you review. Now, if you stop there, there would not be any source of passive income. You can notch your game up by composing songs or even teaching other people how to play an instrument by creating an ebook or an audio course, which are suitable for beginners. Places like Clickbank and Paydotcom can be a good platform to launch your offerings.

9. Building A Website

You can create a website and start marketing, advertising or promote all the ideas you might have. There are various types of websites you can build e.g. pictures, blogs, videos, different kinds of items and any other thing you might want to put in website. You can also open a website and then sell it to another person or let it be your own and then advertise products or sites of different clients and get some cash.

Passive Income Potential (Moderate): You can package your knowledge of website design to sell as ebook or provide retainer service to website owners.

10. Selling Photos

Through selling stock photography in the internet, one can be able to earn a lot of money and this is mainly because the demand is high and the number of media and commercial outlets has highly increased. Growth and advancement of online media has resulted to increase in demand of stock photography that are of high quality.

If you have photography skills you can sell your stock photos online on websites such as Dreamstime, Fotolia, istockphoto, Shutterstock and creativemarket. Your photos are great and all you have to do is give it a try because there are many people who need different kinds of photos for different purposes. You can also do some research and find out photos that people like or are demanding and then start taking them and selling them.

Passive Income Potential (High): A picture paints a thousand words. Once you snap a good photograph, passive income potential is high as you can enjoy royalty from the photo for many years to come.

11. Forex/Stock Trading

It may seem a bit risky to join the forex or stock trading, but you can start learning and continue doing research until you get experienced in that area. Once you have grasped everything you need to know about stock exchange, it will be easier for you to be able to exchange stocks or foreign currencies. Their rates usually fluctuates depending on political and economic influences and most importantly the demand and supply in the world. Your aim as a trader is to identify which currency is likely to fall or rise in value against another. The more time you spend investing in forex trading, the more you will earn.

Passive Income Potential (Low): Trading is a very specialized knowledge and you need to have sufficient capital to begin with. However, gains from your trading account can be channeled to stock investments to enjoy passive dividend income.

12. Searching The Web

It is one of the easiest methods of earning money without much struggle or changing your habit. There are certain websites that pay if you search in Bing, Google or Yahoo and one of them is Qmee.com. You are just required to install an add-on to your browser and then as you search for anything, some supported results might emerge alongside your normal search.

In Qmee.com, every result has a cash payment attached to it and if you like, you can select it and pick your reward. There isn't any limitation to the least amount of money you can withdraw and it has other options of donating your payment to charity.

Passive Income Potential (Low): Not much passive income potential there but hey, getting paid to do some simple tasks is not too bad, ain't it?

13. Writing Articles For Publications

For all those with a passion in journalism or have worked in the field they can try submitting articles to publications as a way of making income online. Don't just wake up one day and randomly write any article, you must have a plan and contact information of the publication company where you want to submit your article to.

Nowadays there are publications of almost all the niches you can think of and some of the publications that hire include; Writing.com, PoeWar Freelance Jobs or Online Writing Jobs.

Passive Income Potential (Moderate): Most people overlook the passive income component of writing. You don't just stop at writing. There is nothing stopping you from bundling your work into packs of private label rights products that can be sold to different clients over and over again. Now that is truly passive income.

14. YouTube

If you are a comedian, filmmaker or a musician and want a large number of audiences, you can simply upload yourself on YouTube. When an ad is displayed in your page, you will be able to earn some cash and this process is the same as pay per click advertising program which is common to other blogs or websites and the sites that can be helpful include Mediaflix and Flixya. Research has been done and it was found that many people usually watch videos on YouTube than they do on Google searches.

Passive Income Potential (Moderate): Similar to blogging, you got to be really good at making videos to be able to make some passive income from it. Once you have established yourself as a youtube celebrity of some sorts, you will get to earn for each click on the ads showing on your videos without you having to do anything. More views on your videos equal more passive income. However, there are some initial effort involved to build a personal brand.

15. Interviewing People

Do you desire or have a dream of taking a career in Human Resource? Do you know how or like asking questions? If the answer for the above questions is "Yes" then you can be hired by some companies that usually pay people for spending their time interviewing other people.

Some companies might cover your travelling cost and then pay you over £180 for conducting an interview but you have to commit over 20 hours per week, if you are good at interviewing people visit NatCen.

You can also learn and understand the pain point people usually experience and then try to interview experts and ask questions about those people who experience the problem. After you have found all the answers you can build a website and start selling the interview, but it is of importance for you to know where you are going to advertise it and be patient.

Passive Income Potential (High): This is the key to making quality products without knowing much about the industry. Simply interview experts in the field and repackage the interview as an audio or home study course. You are leveraging on the expert's brand and knowledge to build a recurring source of income.

16. Transcription

Transcription is mainly found in the medical field and involves making some written copies of materials that are oral dictated by medical experts. These might include clinical notes, psychiatric evaluation, reports, physical and history report, letters, consultation notes and so on.

The spoken words must be transcribed quickly and accurately, this is the most challenging part of the job. For you to be a medical transcriptionist, you should have excellent information and understanding of medical terminology and an accurate and high typing speed. If you get an easy job, you can't earn more but it is the fastest way you can make some money. Sign up on Up-work or e-Lance and start to advertise your services.

Passive Income Potential (Low): You are only getting paid for each transcription service you provide. However, you can try linking up with reputable medical or law firms so you can continue offering your service to them on a monthly retainer basis.

17. "Get Paid To (GPT)" Programme

GPT sites are becoming more popular among youths. You earn by simply playing games, websites, newsletters or even filling out surveys. If you don't have a skill set and you want to earn extra cash then this is suitable for you. If you are interested in taking online surveys, you can register with a few legit, paid survey sites and start answering questions. The topics can range from politics to shopping.

Passive Income Potential (Low): Mostly one off payments for tasks that do not require a lot of specialized skills.

18. Help In Developing An Online Presence Of Local Businesses

Many local businesses struggle and they might have websites but they aren't getting any good result from them, others don't have any website at all. Start by knowing all about search engine optimization, how you can set up email list and then how you are going to apply these for local businesses.

If you normally hang around web marketers, nerds or even web 2.0 crowds, you may come to realize that many owners of businesses are 7 or more behind you. If you can deliver good results, business owners can easily pay you.

Passive Income Potential (High): Most local businesses are not tech savvy and this is where you step in. Offer services such as social campaign management, web design, blogging etc and they will reward you with a handsome monthly retainer fee. Plus, it does not take a lot of time to build and maintain an online presence for local businesses.

19. Making Themes

Lots of people seek online presence and this has lead to an increase in Blog (Word-Press) themes and Website templates. If you are good at coding and Web designing, you can earn a lot of cash from designing Web themes.

In this section, there are typical Websites, which include ThemeForest and TemplateMonster, which is a place where you can market and sell your themes. Templates are normally priced and sold depending on the aspects and rights that are packed with them.

Passive Income Potential (High): You can market your website template as premium products and get paid over and over again for each user who downloads your web template. Sites like wordpress will never go out of fashion.

20. Betting

Betting is a popular and fast way of making money online without breaking the law. Many people are making a lot of money through betting online and this is mainly because betting is legal, tax free, risk free and you can place your bet from anywhere. It removes the risk because as you bet, you are allowed to bet against or for a given outcome. However, it is of importance for you to keep in mind that people are different and when it comes to betting they will have different experiences.

If you don't enjoy gambling then don't try using it as the main source of income. You should at all times be careful and avoid taking chances because at some point it will change from being a fun thing to being a work thing. Also don't make quit your job or change your lifestyle because of gambling.

Passive Income Potential (Low): Again, channel your earnings to stock investments to gain from passive dividend income.

Chapter 5: Ten Tips on Making Money Online More Effectively

Working from a virtual office rather than the physical work location is becoming more popular. Some people spend some time in an actual office, but they may spend some portion of their working week doing online jobs at different locations e.g. from home, in a cafe etc.

Online job is a type of job that allows us to be more mobile and gives us great flexibility more than the traditional methods of working.

If you want to succeed in online jobs there are a number of tips you can master for you to maintain consistency and earn more as you work. Some of the common tips are as explained on the next page:-

Working for different sites

If you want to increase your income try working for different online job sites. Make sure you maintain all of them properly and provide excellent services. This is a good way of learning more new skills because you will be handling many clients who will give you different types of tasks.

Have a back up

If you want to excel working online, you must have reliable tools that can help you to complete your work and also submit it on time. Even if you have the best computer, it is of importance to have a backup plan in place. If you really want to succeed working online and avoid any stress then it is vital to have a plan for a backup technology. You can have a desktop, laptop, iPad, email etc as your backup technology.

Setting up an email address

For you to be up-to-date with your work information you must setup a dedicated email address, so that you can be able to receive all updates through email. In order to avoid some emails that come with scam, make sure the email you have setup is specifically for online jobs.

Storage of money

It is of importance for you to withdraw the money you earn online immediately. This is mainly because online earnings accounts are not banks and they have no protection if the company happens to close. As soon as the payment reaches threshold you should withdraw your cash.

Set aside time to work

The main reason why many people prefer working online is that it is very flexible. By setting aside a period of the day doing online job can help you to plan and manage other responsibilities, such as hobbies, work, family etc. Always be organized and honest with yourself and set aside working hours to avoid emails and phone calls without interfering with your personal time.

Be patient

It is of importance for you to exercise patience. Don't expect to work today and expect to start earning immediately. It usually takes time for you to earn and patience is of importance for you to succeed.

Set aside a place to do your work

While the flexibility of where you do your work is a real draw, setting aside a place for handling tasks of different clients can help build a healthy work and life balance. You can go to a library, a local park or even your house to complete a given task and this can help to reduce guilt, set boundaries and increase productivity.

Meeting deadlines

When a client gives you a certain task, it is your responsibility to make sure that you meet the deadlines and this will assist you to create a good working relationship.

Utilize The Power of Social Media

Take advantage of social networks and community forums for you to be able to0 learn, share ideas and understand more about other online job opportunities.

Maintain Your Professionalism

Don't give out too much professional or sensitive information because some online companies may be fraud.

Chapter 6: Common Mistakes Newbies Make

There are so many mistakes that many people who work online make and that these mistakes can easily be made by beginners. There are also many things happening online and you will most probably come across all sorts of ideas and every type of people you don't know.

If you want to grow and excel in your online income job, then you have to understand what usually happens there and the very common mistakes that you are likely to make. Through knowing this you will be able to create transparency in your mind and be able to face all the challenges and also difficulties. Some mistakes can be minor while others can be major and might end up costing you a lot.

In fact, when competition for opportunities increases the chances that you will make any mistake can make you miss out on a lot of available opportunities. For to be on the safe side it is vital that you keep in mind some of the common mistakes that you can avoid as you struggle to make online income which crucial for you.

It is therefore very important for you to analyze all the possible mistakes for you to be able to avoid making them. Explained below are some common mistakes that are usually made:-

Not having a proper plan

Plan is very important if you really want to perform effectively, deliver quality services and succeed. Planning or scheduling your work properly allows you to allocate time to every task at hand and you are also able to prioritize which are the most urgent tasks and the least urgent ones. Clients prefer people who can provide quality work and meet deadlines, therefore, for you to ensure that you maintain a good working relationship with clients you have to put an effort of planning your work.

Not knowing your value

There are so many people working online and don't know their worth. They might have all the required skills and expertise but might still be underrating their worth. At first, when many people join online jobs they normally offer cheap prices for their services. It is of importance for you to understand that many clients are looking for quality work and they don't mind paying more for good quality work. Start valuing yourself according to the quality of work you produce but not underrating or exaggerating your worth.

Lack of effective networking

For you to be able to know, learn and understand what is available in relation to jobs that can be found online and also for you to expand your career online then you must make networking to be a habit. Networking can help you to expand your field of knowledge.

Lack of clear application

When applying for a job online you must be clear on what your skills, qualifications, specialization and experience. Avoid sending long, disorganized applications but try to be specific about the job you are applying for and what how you can deliver your services.

Not marketing yourself

If you really want to get out there and create a name, you should be able to market yourself by explaining through social media the uniqueness, qualifications and skills that you have and that can attract potential clients or that can make you stand out.

Applying for jobs that are not suitable for you

Before applying for a job online you should make sure you keenly read through the job post and know what the client is looking for. This will give you an opportunity of deciding if it is in line with your qualifications, skills, experience and determine whether it is where you have specialized in. If the job doesn't match your skills and qualifications and you still apply and get hired, you might fail to deliver the required quality work.

Reusing your cover letter

With online jobs you can find professionals/clients interacting with each other on regular basis and they might share information about potential applicants and yours might end up being one of those. If you have been reusing the same cover letter it may affect your growth and hold you back from landing on the job you desire.

Undermining yourself

If you keep on maintaining the mentality that you aren't skilled or good enough to handle things that you know very well you can handle well then it will be quite hard for you to land on a job you are qualified for. Apply for jobs that you know very well you can handle them and that you have specialized in. Don't limit yourself to opportunities because of self doubt and negativity but let the client decide that.

Not researching on potential clients

If you want to confirm if a job is legitimate or a scam and whether it is what you can do or not then you should carry out a good research on them. This will help you to make the appropriate decision regarding what the employers have to offer. This will also help you to decide if it is what you can do or not.

Showing your disappointment online

No matter what you have been through in life there is no need to put your frustrations online and you should keep in mind that no client owes you a job online. If you applied for an online job and it happens that you have gotten it then that is great and if you don't get it, don't give up but exercise patience, try harder and avoid having negative attitude towards clients or online companies.

Chapter 7: Developing The Right Mindset For Success

To make it in whatever area of life you have to ensure that you build a mindset for success and allow this to be your strength and source of motivation.

It is through the power of thought and mind that we get to places we want to be in life or even achieve the best of what life holds. Being able to establish a specific way of thinking about life will highly help you achieve your dreams.

As you plan to make a breakthrough with online income then you should know that with effort and perseverance you can be able to broaden your skills, expand your intellect, improve character and overcome obstacles. That growth mindset is what you will need especially to achieve your financial goals and dreams.

What you should always have in mind is the fact that when you change your inner game you change your outer game. The key thing is that when you change your thoughts it changes how you feel giving you room for more advanced thoughts.

One finds it easier to take action when they are feeling good and as you know action determines results. It is never easy to take risks in life unless you have inner strength to do so which is determined by mindset.

Life is all a struggle and much of what we achieve is highly linked to our thoughts and feelings. If today you have made the decision of working online then you will need to feel great about the idea before you even begin because that is where the best source of inspiration lies.

Research has proved that every single person, whether young or old is at a risk of succumbing to a fixed. We only grow when we allow our minds to grow; if you want to something then you should start by believing in that possibility because doubts and fear break you.

Sometimes it's not all about skills and qualifications but all you may need is just the right mindset. So many times I have gone for job interviews with a specific mindset, that being the fact that I may not be as qualified as other candidates and that I will never get that job and I never did.

This is because I had already decided my fate and thus lacked the strength to try harder and prove myself wrong. Sometimes we are just as good as they want us to be but we can't admit that to ourselves.

There is a place for anyone in this life and whatever you are struggling to achieve will only be made possible if you decide to work on growing or changing your mindset. All life is a struggle and the challenges we come across are what make the journey interesting and of value.

Talent is important but it should not be what you use to determine your success because there is so much to it. What you should always do as a person is align all your thoughts with the growth mindset.

According to Debbie Millman, "If you imagine less, less will be what you undoubtedly deserve." This is so because the first step to acquiring the things you want in life is through believing that you actually deserve them.

We all have different goals that we are pursuing and this makes it very important for you to develop the growth mindset and this gives you a more flexible view on success.

With this kind of mindset you will also adapt to the habit of viewing failure as a starting point for experimentation and not as a reflection of their abilities.

With a fixed mindset you will always tend to believe that character, intelligence and creative potential are unchangeable traits and can therefore not be modified in any way which is wrong.

As you plan to make income online you should know that it is not easy because you will need to put effort to gain the much you want. This is why you will need the kind of mindset that will take you to a higher step from time to time and allow you to grow as a person and also financially because this is what we all strive for in life.

It is not an easy path to break that online millionaire code but when you put your all to it then I assure you it will be more than possible. Allow yourself to adjust to the difficulties and challenges in life and you will learn to be mentally strong no matter how difficult things appear to be.

As you know, no one will change your life for and this makes it your responsibility to grasp all the knowledge you gain and use it to change your life for the better.

The great things in life are not limited to a chosen group of people and we all have a chance at it as long as we maintain the right mindset. We all want to be successful and happy in life, whether you have business, home or family goals they can all be achieved when you set your mindset for success.

Chapter 8: Quotes from Successful People to Keep You Motivated

Sometimes, it is really difficult to find the motivation to succeed in your online passive income endeavors. Thus, I have dedicated one whole chapter to feed your mind with quotes from successful people who have found their wealth online so you will have the drive and motivation to keep going when things get tough.

Always remember that there is always hope and light at the end of the tunnel. So here goes:

Quotes from Jeff Walker, a product launch guru

"At its heart, Product Launch Formula is made up of sequences, stories, and triggers."

"Our product launches use a series of sequences—pre-prelaunch, the prelaunch, the launch, and the post-launch."

"Your most scarce resource is focus."

"Making the right decisions around that opportunity cost is one of the biggest factors in the success of your business."

"If you want to make your business and your marketing memorable, then your marketing needs to tell a story."

Quotes from T Harv Eker, Secrets of The Millionaire Mind

"If you want to change the fruits, you will first have to change the roots. If you want to change the visible, you must first change the invisible."

"If you are willing to do only what's easy, life will be hard. But if you are willing to do what's hard, life will be easy."

"If you are insecure, guess what? The rest of the world is too. Do not overestimate the competition and underestimate yourself. You are better than you think."

"If you shoot for the stars, you'll at least hit the moon"

"If your motivation for acquiring money or success comes from a nonsupportive root such as fear, anger, or the need to "prove" yourself, your money will never bring you happiness."

Quotes from Brendon Burchard, The Millionaire Messenger

"No matter your position, circumstances, or opportunities in life, you always have the freedom of mind to choose how you experience, interpret, and, ultimately, shape your world."

"You are a child of God, and that alone makes you worthy of care and love. If your guard is up, let it down. If you've constructed a defensive wall to protect yourself and keep all the bad guys out, don't forget who that wall also prevents from getting in—the good guys."

"We must set intentions for who we are, for what roles we wish to serve, for how we'll relate with the world. Without a vibrant awareness, we cannot connect with others or ourselves, nor can we meet the demands of the hour with grace. For this, we now declare: WE SHALL MEET LIFE WITH FULL PRESENCE AND POWER."

"We learn that the more we are true to ourselves, the more we can connect with and contribute to the world."

Quotes from Nick Vjucic, Life Without Limits

"If I fail, I try again, and again, and again. If YOU fail, are you going to try again? The human spirit can handle much worse than we realize. It matters HOW you are going to FINISH. Are you going to finish strong?"

"It's a lie to think you're not good enough. It's a lie to think you're not worth anything."

"I never met a bitter person who was thankful. Or a thankful person who was bitter."

"We can't, and we should not, compare sufferings. We come together as a family of God, hand in hand. And then together coming and standing upon the promises of God, knowing that no matter who you are, no matter what you're going through, that God knows it, He is with you, He is going to pull you through."

".. Fear is often described as False Evidence Appearing Real."

Quotes from Andrew Matthews, Happiness in A Nutshell

"Whenever we doubt our own ability to achieve, it is worthwile pondering the obstacles that others have overcome.   To   name   a   few...
*Napoleon overcame his considerable handicap, his tiny stature, to lead his conquering armies across Europe.
*Abraham Lincon failed in business aged 31, lost a legislative race and 32, again failed in business at 34, had his sweetheart die when he was 35, had a nervous breakdown at 36, lost congressional races aged 43, 46 and 48, lost a senatorial race at 55, failed in his efforts to become vice president of the U.S.A aged 56 and lost a further senatorial contest at 58. At 60 years of age he was elected president of the U.S.A and is now remembered as one of the great leaders in world history.
*Winston Churchill was a poor student with a speech impediment. Not only did he win a Nobel Prize at 24, but he became one of the most inspiring speakers of recent times.
It is not where you start that counts, but where you choose to finish."

"It's not what happens to you that determines your happiness. It's how you think about what happens to you."

"Whatever thoughts are causing you pain, they are only thoughts. You can change a thought."

Special Bonus

To thank you for purchasing my guide, I would like to give you free access to the Easypreneur membership area, which I had created together with my partners Dave and Imran. You will receive over $997 worth of moneymaking gifts:

Inside the membership area, you will find:

1. 5 Creative Ways to Turn a $7 report into a $197 order so you can make more money from an existing digital product

2. 52 Ways to Create Special Promotional Offers to get your potential buyers salivating even before they open their wallet

3. And many more....

To get access to your membership area, simply visit the URL below:

http://licensetoprofits.com

....And put in both your name and email there so I know who to address and which email address to send your membership information to

Conclusion

I hope this book was able to help you have a deeper understanding of online income, allowed you to know where you can start from and most importantly helped you to have an idea of what kind of online job you can do. There are other types of online jobs out there and the book just explained a few of them, once you begin looking for online jobs you might find something great that is suitable for you.

-- Ken Chong

www.ingramcontent.com/pod-product-compliance
Lightning Source LLC
Chambersburg PA
CBHW070908180526
45168CB00005B/1968